# A MONTH OF HOPE

## Your Five-Minute Daily Pick-Me-Up

### Dr. Mark Eckart

# A MONTH OF HOPE

**Your Five-Minute Daily Pick-Me-Up**

## Dr. Mark Eckart

"Thanks to Dr. Mark Eckart for this thirty-day devotional, *A Month of Hope*. In the hectic pace of our daily lives, this can prove helpful in bringing our focus on matters of eternal substance. These Scriptures, with Dr. Mark's comments, thoughts, and reflections, will assist in doing that."

DR. KEN FARMER
*Managing Editor,* God's Revivalist
*God's Bible School & College*

"What a refreshing devotional book Dr. Eckart has written. From its cover page to its last page, you will be inspired and uplifted with its message of hope. In a world of uncertainty, the stories and Scriptures that are woven together are a blessed reminder that the uncertainty of this world matters very little when we discover that the hope we find in Jesus is all we need."

REV. MICHAEL STOELTING
*Assistant District Superintendent*
*Indiana South Wesleyan District, The Wesleyan Church*

*A Month of Hope*

ISBN 978-1-948362-26-9

Copyright © 2019
All rights reserved. No part of this publication (except for Bible verses) may be reproduced or used in any form or by any means – graphics, electronic, or mechanical, including photocopying, recording, taping, or information storage or retrieval systems – without prior written permission of the author.

To order more books, you can send an email to eckart84@gmail.com or call 812.865.3979

Note: the word "hope" appears in bold type in Bible verses under "Hopeful Reflections" for the purpose of added emphasis.

# Introduction

Let's face it, we live in a beat-up world. There are wars and rumors of wars, mass killings, natural disasters, and such hate displayed between the races and in the human family. You name it, and it seems this generation has experienced it. Don't we all long for hope – something that will get us beyond our fears of today and insecurities of tomorrow?

Hope. It is something we all need and can't live without very long. One person said it well when they stated, "You can live forty days without food, four days without water, but about four seconds without hope!"

Well, I have great news! We can go to a source given to us outside of our world. In fact, the source is who made us – God Himself. When we turn to the Bible, it is like sitting down and letting God talk to us as we journey through this maze of life.

The best news is God's Word offers us hope all throughout the nearly 1,200 pages of the Bible. The word hope itself is used **166** times in **158** verses in the Bible (NIV), and the idea of hope is on hundreds of pages in this special book.

So, what I do in this devotional is just take a few verses and then comment about those verses to give you hope for each day of the month. My goal is to make them meaningful but short enough that you can read them quickly throughout the day as you wish.

The Psalmist in 33:22 (NKJV) writes about hope when he says, "Let Your mercy, O Lord, be upon us, just as we **hope** in You." My prayer for you is what Apostle Paul wrote in Romans 15:13 (NIV):

> "May the God of **hope** fill you with all joy
> and peace as you trust in him, so
> that you may overflow with
> **hope** by the power of
> the Holy Spirit."

Mark Eckart
September 2019

GENESIS 1:1, 26-28 (NIV)

## You were made by the Holy Trinity

*In the beginning God created the heavens and the earth.*

*Then God said, "Let us make mankind in our image, in our likeness, so that they may rule over the fish in the sea and the birds in the sky, over the livestock and all the wild animals, and over all the creatures that move along the ground." So God created mankind in his own image, in the image of God he created them; male and female he created them. God blessed them and said to them, "Be fruitful and increase in number; fill the earth and subdue it. Rule over the fish in the sea and the birds in the sky and over every living creature that moves on the ground."*

Isn't it comforting to know that God made us? Most scholars believe that when it says, "Let Us" in verse 26 that it is talking about the Holy Trinity. Wow! Rejoice today that you resemble God.

My oldest child is the only son I've got. More than once I have heard people say, "You look just like your dad." I think this makes me feel better than him!

You are not God, but you are made in His image. God the Father, the Son, and the Holy Spirit had a part in you being born. You count! You are significant! And if God made you, He loves you! You have His DNA.

*Rejoice today that you resemble God.*

**Thought for the day:**
Since God did not make junk, you are significant and of great worth to Him and others!

GENESIS 3:14 & 15 (NIV)

## Jesus crushes the head of Satan

*So the Lord God said to the serpent, "Because you have done this, Cursed are you above all livestock and all wild animals! You will crawl on your belly and you will eat dust all the days of your life. And I will put enmity between you and the woman, and between your offspring and hers; he will crush your head, and you will strike his heel."*

In verse 15, the serpent represents Satan. It is believed by many that it's the first verse in the Bible to reference Jesus specifically. Since we believe that is the case, did you catch the good news?

Notice the language in 15, "He will crush your head." Satan is being told for the first time that even though he won the battle in the Garden of Eden (enticing Adam and Eve to sin), he will NOT win the final war.

Proof of this is that Jesus was born about 2,000 years ago, died for our sins, and then praise be to God He crushed Satan's head by being resurrected on the third day!

We were in church when I was a boy when suddenly a drunk walked in and before long staggered down to the altar and wanted to pray. The minister and a few members gathered around to show concern and pray for him.

We found out his name was John. He had traveled the world over serving in the US Air Force but still did not find happiness. *The bottle had gotten the best of him, and he was an alcoholic.* But now John was in the church seeking help.

That night John asked forgiveness for his sins and found the peace of God through Christ that passes ALL understanding, as the Bible says. I was amazed as a kid at the difference salvation made in John. He became a faithful church member who was there every time the doors were open. John became a new man in Christ and was faithful until he died. In other words, Jesus crushed the head of Satan in John's life!

**Thought for the Day:**
Be hopeful for today because Jesus has already won the battle, and he knows how to be a head crusher to Satan in your life!

**Hopeful Reflections:**

> *Therefore my heart is glad, and my glory rejoices; my flesh also will rest in* **hope** (Psalm 16:9, NKJV).

> Once you choose hope, anything's possible.
> —*Christopher Reeve*

GENESIS 5:21 – 24 (NIV)

# Walking faithfully with God

*When Enoch had lived 65 years, he became the father of Methuselah. After he became the father of Methuselah, Enoch walked faithfully with God 300 years and had other sons and daughters. Altogether, Enoch lived a total of 365 years. Enoch walked faithfully with God; then he was no more, because God took him away.*

This chapter talks about genealogies and lists of people. Boring, right? But wait a minute, don't miss something found in verses 22 and 24 above: Enoch walked faithfully with God.

Do you want to be filled with hope today? Then make it a habit daily to walk with God in communion and fellowship. He loves you as His child and can't wait for you to walk and talk with Him!

Don't you long for that walking and communion with God? Sure you do, because we are all born to be on that spiritual journey trying to get back home.

When I was about 14, I got a new 10-speed bicycle. It was yellow, and man was it fast! My friend Tim and I used to ride miles on our bikes. There was a lady at our church that we respectfully called "Granny Fay." She loved for us to stop by her home, which was a several miles ride from where we would start. She loved the company, and we loved the cold 16 oz Pepsi (bottle they sold back then) waiting for us to drink.

*Don't you long for that walking and communion with God?*

Sometimes, though, when we would walk up on her porch, we could hear her praying in her living room. When that happened, even though Tim and I would be craving a cold Pepsi on a hot summer day, we wouldn't dare bother her prayer time because we knew this saint of God was communing with her God! We would go on our way and hopefully get that cold Pepsi the next time through.

**Thought for the day:**
You will find no closer friend to walk and communicate with than God!

**Hopeful Reflections:**

> *Be of good courage, and He shall strengthen your heart, all you who **hope** in the Lord* (Psalm 31:24, NKJV).

> Most of the important things in the world have been accomplished by people who have kept on trying when there seemed to be no hope at all. —*Dale Carnegie*

GENESIS 6:8 (NKJV)

# Finding grace (favor) in God's sight

*So the Lord said, "I will destroy man whom I have created from the face of the earth, both man and beast, creeping thing and birds of the air, for I am sorry that I have made them." But Noah found grace in the eyes of the Lord.*

As we know from the earlier part of Genesis, God made humans, and then they sinned and messed up His original plan. They sinned so much that God was deeply grieved and was planning to destroy man but then hope showed up! So, in verse eight we see that Noah found grace (favor) in the eyes of the Lord.

My great grandfather (four greats ago) was a minister who preached Abraham Lincoln's mother's funeral. My cousin Harold and I went to visit Rev. David Elkins' grave site. On the way back to our car, I looked down and saw a roll of money lying in the leaves. Since a lot of tourists see his grave, I didn't have a clue whose money it was. I took it and bought our lunch. I told Harold that day that it does pay to go see Grandpa!

> *My great grandfather (four greats ago) was a minister who preached Abraham Lincoln's mother's funeral.*

I found only money, but Noah found grace! Money can buy your lunch to fill your tummy, but grace can provide forgiveness, hope, joy, and peace to fill your soul. When Noah found grace, "undeserved favor" with God, it changed his life for better and forever.

God is still giving out grace. Go ahead and ask Him, it will change your life as well.

**Thought for the day:**
As it has been said, grace is "God's riches at Christ's expense." You cannot earn the grace of God, but you can certainly receive and enjoy it!

**Hopeful Reflections:**

> *But the eyes of the Lord are on those who fear him, on those whose **hope** is in his unfailing love* (Psalm 33:18, NIV).
>
> Without Christ there is no hope.
> —*Charles Spurgeon*

 Genesis 9:12, 13, & 15 (NIV)

## A promise in the sky

*And God said, "This is the sign of the covenant I am making between me and you and every living creature with you, a covenant for all generations to come: I have set my rainbow in the clouds, and it will be the sign of the covenant between me and the earth.... Never again will the waters become a flood to destroy all life."*

An atheist says there is no God, and an agnostic doubts there is a God. However, to believe in God takes faith. No doubt you have had some doubts concerning your faith; I know I have at times.

It takes faith to believe a chair will hold you up when you sit down, that your money will be safe in the bank, and that the doctor knows what she is doing when you get that prescription filled. But it also takes faith to believe that God made us, is in control of the universe, and is watching out for us.

Don't miss the ray of hope shining through in the verses quoted above that can help boost our faith. One of the biggest proofs there is a God is the rainbow.

> *One of the biggest proofs there is a God is the rainbow.*

When my children were small and a rainbow would appear after the rain, I would use it as a teaching moment. I would say, "Look, kids, that is God in heaven telling us, 'I'm still up here, and look at my sign that I promised to never flood the whole earth again.'"

**Thought for the day:**
The next time you see that beautiful arc of majestic colors glistening in the sky, take hope in the fact that God is alive and well! The rainbow is a covenant for *all generations,* which includes us.

GENESIS 15:1 (NIV)

## Do not be afraid

*After this, the word of the Lord came to Abram in a vision: "Do not be afraid, Abram. I am your shield, your very great reward."*

What do you fear today? The devil tries every tactic to make us all scared. He wants us to fret away today by worrying about what we did wrong yesterday and being overly concerned about all the bad things that may happen tomorrow. Notice I said, "may." Most of the things we worry about don't happen.

Abram (later to be named Abraham) can relate. He was fearful that he would go childless and therefore need to give his inheritance to an adopted son to carry on his name. But God had other plans. In verse five of Genesis chapter fifteen, He had Abram to scan the heavens; and He told him his offspring would be as many as the number of stars you could see on a pitch-dark night!

A pastor friend of mine was afraid. While serving as the District Superintendent, I asked him to pastor a church that was really struggling. He told me he didn't feel led to do so. But then he called me back and said God gave him a vision and showed him all the good things that would happen at that church. Of course, I was thankful; and it is amazing what has taken place at the church since my pastor friend moved to that setting: New people are attending, they have spent $90,000.00 on renovations (with no debt), and families are being reached with the good news of Christ.

> *Most of the things we worry about don't happen.*

**Thought for the day:**
Listen for that voice of God today as He says to you, "Do not be afraid (say your name!)." God is the best antidote for fear!

**Hopeful Reflections:**

> *May your unfailing love be with us, LORD, even as we put our **hope** in you* (Psalm 33:22, NIV).

God is the only one who can make the valley of trouble a door of hope.
—*Catherine Marshall*

# Day 7

GENESIS 18: 13 & 14 (NIV)

## Nothing is too hard for the Lord

*Then the Lord said to Abraham, "Why did Sarah laugh and say, 'Will I really have a child, now that I am old?' Is anything too hard for the Lord? I will return to you at the appointed time next year, and Sarah will have a son."*

Let's be honest, we have all had our chuckling moments when it looked like there was no way that God could do the impossible. No doubt Sarah laughed thinking about the idea of her having a baby at age 90!

I'm sure she thought that parents have babies, not grandparents. She snickered, probably thinking of her husband, Abraham, nearly 100 years old playing hide and seek with their child in a few years! You get the idea. It seemed ridiculous until God got involved.

That is how it is with us. We have mountains to climb, problems to solve, and crises to face; but then God shows up!

> *My friend Pastor Bob was diagnosed with stage four cancer.*

My friend Pastor Bob was diagnosed with stage four cancer. I was at the doctor's office with him when the surgeon said, "You have a very aggressive form of cancer in the last stages. I need to operate soon; and even then, your chances of living are slim." Wow, that was a shocking diagnosis.

Many of his friends started praying and believing for his healing. So, God did show up and healed him. That same doctor, about three weeks after the first, visit called Bob at home and commented, "Bob, we have a miracle here. We don't understand it, but your cancer is ALL gone!" That has been eight years, and he is still cancer free.

**Thought for the day:**
Your situation may seem insurmountable with no way out; but dwell on this question, "Is anything too hard for the Lord?" We know, of course, nothing is too hard for Him. He can give grandma a baby if He chooses to!

**Hopeful Reflections:**

> *Yet this I call to mind and therefore I have* **hope:** *Because of the Lord's great love we are not consumed, for his compassions never fail* (Lamentations 3:21-22, NIV).

Hope is the thing with feathers that perches in the soul and sings the tune without the words—and never stops at all.
—*Emily Dickinson*

# Day 8

GENESIS 19: 15 & 16 (NIV)

## Angels can rescue you

*With the coming of dawn, the angels urged Lot, saying, "Hurry! Take your wife and your two daughters who are here, or you will be swept away when the city is punished." When he hesitated, the men grasped his hand and the hands of his wife and of his two daughters and led them safely out of the city, for the Lord was merciful to them.*

God was upset because there was so much sin and degradation in the cities of Sodom and Gomorrah. He had given them chance after chance and had been more than fair with the rebellious residents of these cities. Judgment was coming, and Lot (Abraham's nephew) and his family were in danger of losing their lives.

However, because of God's mercy, He sent two angels to drag them to safety! Dr. Billy Graham wrote a whole book about angels; and the Bible has a lot to say about angels, even suggesting that we have a guardian angel (see Psalm 91:11).

As a boy, I got to know Mr. Barnes. He was the commander of a tank in the Korean War. In the heat of a battle, he promised God that if he got back home safely, he would serve him all the days of his life, which he did.

*About that time a huge bomb went off right where his tank would have been if he would have moved!*

One day, while they were fighting, his commanding officer told him to pull his tank forward. Mr. Barnes tried to, but it wouldn't go in gear. It had been working fine previously. This happened several times, and finally the commanding officer screamed, "Barnes, I told you to pull forward." Mr. Barnes replied, "Sir, I am trying." About that time a huge bomb went off right where his tank would have been if he would have moved! In his case, no doubt his guardian angel jammed the gears so his tank would not move.

**Thought for the day:**
Ask God for His protection and help. Your guardian angel can rescue you in many ways!

**Hopeful Reflections:**

> *Why, my soul, are you downcast? Why so disturbed within me? Put your **hope** in God, for I will yet praise him, my Savior and my God* (Psalm 42:11, NIV).

The best we can hope for in this life is a knothole peek at the shining realities ahead. Yet a glimpse is enough. It's enough to convince our hearts that whatever sufferings and sorrows currently assail us aren't worthy of comparison to that which waits over the horizon.
—*Joni Eareckson Tada*

# Day 9

GENESIS 24: 12, 14, & 19 (NIV)

## God will speak to you, sometimes directly

*Then he prayed, "Lord, God of my master Abraham, make me successful today, and show kindness to my master Abraham. May it be that when I say to a young woman, 'Please let down your jar that I may have a drink,' and she says, 'Drink, and I'll water your camels too'—let her be the one you have chosen for your servant Isaac. By this, I will know that you have shown kindness to my master." After she had given him a drink, she said, "I'll draw water for your camels too, until they have had enough to drink."*

In the account above, Abraham had sent his servant back to his homeland of Mesopotamia to find his son Isaac a wife. In the process, the servant didn't want to blow this deal (after all, he is choosing a wife for someone else!).

So, the servant prayed specifically that God would speak to the prospective wife to make this offer without being asked to do so when he approached her, "I'll draw water for your camels too until they have had enough to drink." Guess what. Rebekah did it, and later she became Isaac's wife.

Not all the time by any means, but God can still speak in our spirits almost verbally at times. What hope we have that the creator will communicate with the created! This has happened to me; and at times I have obeyed God, and sometimes, unfortunately, I have not. When I don't, it never works out right.

*One day I felt im-pressed to offer to buy a family their lunch.*

One day I felt impressed to offer to buy a family their lunch. I first resisted but then finally obeyed. When I mentioned my plans to them, one of the family members started crying. They were not tears of embarrassment but joy. What I found out was that earlier that day they were concerned because they had no money to buy food for lunch, and my offer was an answer to prayer for them. It was a win-win situation. I felt humbled to meet their need, and they were overjoyed to have money for food.

**Thought for the day:**
Be listening, because God will be communicating with you, sometimes specifically; and He always has your best interest at heart.

**Hopeful Reflections:**

> *For You are my **hope**, O Lord God; You are my trust from my youth* (Psalm 71:5, NKJV).

Hope begins in the dark, the stubborn hope that if you just show up and try to do the right thing, the dawn will come. You wait and watch and work: You don't give up.
—*Anne Lamott*

 Genesis 37:24 & 28 (NKJ)

## God can get you out of a pit

*Then they took him (Joseph) and cast him into a pit. And the pit was empty; there was no water in it. Then Midianite traders passed by; so, the brothers pulled Joseph up and lifted him out of the pit, and sold him to the Ishmaelites for twenty shekels of silver. And they took Joseph to Egypt.*

It looked like Joseph was finished. His jealous brothers had thrown him into a pit hoping he would die. They were mad at him because he could properly interpret dreams and they perceived that he was their father's favorite son. Notice the pit had no water; just thinking about it makes me thirsty!

God had other plans, though. His brothers put him in the waterless pit, but they did use better judgment and decided to sell him to a group of travelers from Midian. Even then it didn't look promising for Joseph, because they sold him as a slave.

Little did they know that God was using this as a starting point to elevate Joseph to the second highest (only Pharaoh himself was above him) in Egypt. God took him from a waterless pit to an Egyptian palace where he had everything at his disposal.

God still gets people out of pits. My friend, Skip, was in a pit of sin and despair so addicted to drugs that he went 28 days straight without sleeping. He started to deal in drugs, and one day he counted that he had $35,000.00 cash on him. Many of his supposed friends died because a drug deal went bad. But not Skip!

*God still gets people out of pits.*

He came to know Christ, got delivered from his bad habits of alcoholism and drug use, and is now a minister for Christ helping others to be rescued from the pit!

**Thought for the day:**
What pit are you in today? Is it depression, loneliness, debt, health issues, a spiritual problem? Take heart, my friend, because God is still getting people out of pits. Just ask Him to help you today!

**Hopeful Reflections:**

> *But I will **hope** continually, and will praise You yet more and more* (Psalm 71:14, NKJV).

What gives me the most hope every day is God's grace; knowing that his grace is going to give me the strength for whatever I face, knowing that nothing is a surprise to God.
—*Rick Warren*

## Day 11 — Genesis 40:14, 15, & 23 (NIV)

# People will disappoint you, but God won't

*[Joseph said:] "But when all goes well with you, remember me and show me kindness; mention me to Pharaoh and get me out of this prison. I was forcibly carried off from the land of the Hebrews, and even here I have done nothing to deserve being put in a dungeon. The chief cupbearer, however, did not remember Joseph; he forgot him."*

If anyone had a "right" to get bitter, it seems Joseph did. His brothers rejected him and sold him into slavery. When he got to Egypt, his boss's wife became flirtatious with him; and when he rejected her advances, she accused him of wanting to have sex with her.

The wife convinced her husband Potiphar that Joseph was sexually promiscuous with her, so off to prison Joseph went. He was sent to prison and was later able to interpret a couple of dreams accurately for two new-found prison friends (the chief baker and chief butler) who were in prison because Pharaoh had gotten angry at them.

> *Even though Joseph could not see it, God was still working be-hind the scenes.*

The butler and baker eventually got out of prison, and as they were on the way out the door Joseph said, "Hey, mention me to Pharaoh so I can get out of this prison." Of course, they forget him; and it was two full years (or hundreds of days later) before Joseph got out of prison. Wow—what friends!

Even though Joseph could not see it, God was still working behind the scenes. Little did he know that in a couple of years he would be released from prison and become the second highest government leader in Egypt!

This reminds me of another man who went to prison. His name was Chuck Colson. In 1974, Mr. Colson, a former top aide to President Nixon, voluntarily pled guilty to obstruction of justice on a Watergate-related charge and served seven months in Alabama's Maxwell Prison.

In his best-selling memoir, *Born Again*, Chuck wrote: "After I became born again I found myself increasingly drawn to the idea that God had put me in prison for a purpose and that I should do something for those I had left behind."

Colson emerged from prison with a new mission: mobilizing the Christian church to minister to prisoners. He founded Prison Fellowship® in 1976, which has become the nation's largest Christian nonprofit serving prisoners, former prisoners, and their families, and a leading advocate for criminal justice reform. In recognition of his work among prisoners, Colson received the prestigious Templeton Prize for Progress in Religion in 1993.

**Thought for the day:**
Don't get sidetracked by what you can't see! Many times, our trials will turn to triumphs when God gets finished.

**Hopeful Reflections:**

> *You are my hiding place and my shield; I **hope** in Your word* (Psalm 119:114, NKJV).

> Jesus gives us hope because He keeps us company, has a vision and knows the way we should go. —*Max Lucado*

GENESIS 41:39 – 41 (NIV)

# When God opens a door of opportunity

*Then Pharaoh said to Joseph, "Since God has made all this known to you, there is no one so discerning and wise as you. You shall be in charge of my palace, and all my people are to submit to your orders. Only with respect to the throne will I be greater than you." So Pharaoh said to Joseph, "I hereby put you in charge of the whole land of Egypt."*

Joseph had been faithful to God, and now God was faithful to him! Up to this point, the journey for Joseph had not been easy. He had been put in a pit by his brothers because of jealousy and in prison on false allegations by Potiphar's wife.

Yet God, as seen in the verses quoted above, is going to exalt him to be the second highest ranking official in Egypt! Pharaoh was impressed with the wisdom of Joseph, and God was impressed with his humility. Through all the trials that Joseph faced, he stayed humble and holy.

*You just never know when God is going to open a door of oppor-tunity for a person.*

You just never know when God is going to open a door of opportunity for a person. He opens doors for people at times they don't deserve it and haven't even planned for His goodness. He is sovereign, and He does what He wants when He wants.

Take, for example, Debbie Macomber. She is dyslexic and had a learning disorder and didn't start reading until she was ten years old and in the fifth grade. Despite this shaky academic background, she had a dream to write novels.

Finally, the dream got so strong that when she turned thirty, she rented a typewriter, set it up on her kitchen table and started writing. When she received rejection letters about her writings (and she got a boatload of those), she would read another chapter of Dr. Norman Vincent Peale's book, *The Power of Positive Thinking.*

Through her hard work and positive thinking, God opened a door for Debbie the size of Texas! She has published dozens of books, been on national bestseller lists, had movies made about her books, and met thousands of fans at book signings!

**Thought for the day:**
Stay holy and humble because God may open an exciting door for you! God loves to surprise His children with good gifts.

**Hopeful Reflections:**

> *Blessed are those whose help is the God of Jacob, whose **hope** is in the Lord their God* (Psalm 146:5, NIV).
>
> Notice the word "hope" (in Psalm 62:5). The Hebrew term literally means "a cord, as an attachment." Every one of us is hanging on to something or someone for security.... If it's someone or something other than God alone, you're hanging on by a thread—the wrong thread. —*Beth Moore*

## Day 13

GENESIS 45:3B, 4, 5, AND 8 (NIV)

# When bad turns to good

*But his brothers were not able to answer him, because they were terrified at his presence. Then Joseph said to his brothers, "Come close to me." When they had done so, he said, "I am your brother Joseph, the one you sold into Egypt! And now, do not be distressed and do not be angry with yourselves for selling me here, because it was to save lives that God sent me ahead of you. So then, it was not you who sent me here, but God. He made me father to Pharaoh, lord of his entire household and ruler of all Egypt."*

Can you imagine how Joseph's brothers felt when he revealed to them that he was part of the family? Up to this point, they were thinking that Joseph was serving as a slave somewhere or dead for all they knew.

But they were wrong. The kid brothers find themselves standing before Joseph and are terrified remembering how they had mistreated him in the past. Yes, they remember putting him in a dark, dingy pit and selling him to a bunch of vagabonds headed to Egypt. No wonder they are shaking in their boots. They feel as guilty as a drunk driver being approached by a state cop after causing a bad wreck. Joseph now has the authority to make life miserable for them.

*Take hope today, be-cause God often turns what seems to be bad for good.*

But Joseph didn't do that. He calmed their nerves quickly by telling them not to be distressed because it was God that had orchestrated this whole ordeal. Take hope today, because God often turns what seems to be bad for good.

When I was in college, they had a quartet singing group that traveled across the United States representing the school. This was a prestigious gig that not only allowed you to meet many people and see new places, but it also paid your tuition for college. I auditioned for the quartet but did not make it. I was extremely disappointed. Later, I auditioned for and successfully became a part of the college choir. It was a privilege, but being in the choir did not pay your school bill.

However, God had something else in mind! Shortly after I did not make it into the quartet, I was approached about serving as a resident assistant in the men's dormitory. I accepted this position because it also paid my tuition, plus it eventually afforded me a private room so I could study more effectively.

Not only that, but by me serving as a resident assistant this started me on an academic track where I was eventually able (with much hard work and God's help) to earn a couple of master's degrees, a doctorate, plus become vice-president of the college where I graduated! This would never have happened if I was out every weekend singing from Maine to Montana and everywhere in between.

**Thought for today:**
Like Joseph, what appeared to me as bad God was turning into something good. Be on the lookout, because God may be doing that right now in your life as well!

**Hopeful Reflections:**

> *Blessed is the man who trusts in the Lord, and whose **hope** is the Lord* (Jeremiah 17:7, NKJV).

Our world today so desperately hungers for hope, yet uncounted people have almost given up. There is despair and hopelessness on every hand. Let us be faithful in proclaiming the hope that is in Jesus. —*Billy Graham*

Day 14

EXODUS: 2:8 – 10 (NIV)

## One way God shows his love is by providing for us

*"Yes, go," she answered. So the girl went and got the baby's mother. Pharaoh's daughter said to her, "Take this baby and nurse him for me, and I will pay you." So the woman took the baby and nursed him. When the child grew older, she took him to Pharaoh's daughter and he became her son. She named him Moses, saying, "I drew him out of the water."*

There was a new king of Egypt that rose up after Joseph died who did not have an appreciation for the Jewish people who were living there. He was another Pharaoh that came to power, and he was fearful that the Jewish people would multiply to the point that they would overpower the Egyptian folks. Therefore, Pharaoh had ordered all the Hebrew baby boys killed when they were born.

So when Moses, a Hebrew, was born, his mother's love kicked in; and she hid him for three months, so he would not be killed. When she could no longer hide him that way, she built a little ark (boat) with a lid on it and put him at the edge of the Nile River among the tall grass and had his sister to stand watch over him.

*Moses' mother got paid a good wage to raise her own son!*

Of all things, Pharaoh's daughter came down to the Nile River to bathe and saw the boat, and when she opened it she found Moses. Pharaoh's daughter recognized it as one of the Hebrew babies and had compassion on him when he started crying.

About this time Moses' sister walked up and offered to get a Hebrew woman to nurse the baby, to which Pharaoh's daughter agreed. As providence would have it, the sister went and got Moses' mother to nurse and raise him; and besides that, Pharaoh's daughter paid her to do so! A few years later Moses would become the son of Pharaoh's daughter, as she would adopt him; this was also in God's plan.

How can you beat that? Moses' mother got paid a good wage to raise her own son!

My friend Professor Ken worked at a Bible college for decades. He had several kids but not much money. There were eight in the family including the six children. It was time for them to see an optometrist to get their eyes checked.

They had not gone in a couple of years because of lack of finances. When they did decide to go, they prayed, asking God to provide for them in this endeavor. They went to a couple of doctor's offices; but both times when they pulled into the parking lots, they did not feel those were the eye doctors to visit.

They then went to a third place and felt like they should go see that doctor. When they were registering, the form asked the occupation of Professor Ken. He put down he was a teacher at a Bible college and a minister preparing ministers to be in ministry as well.

After the doctor reviewed the information, he came out and said to Ken, "This must be your lucky day!"

"Why do you say that?" responded Ken.

The eye doctor commented, "I promised God if He helped me through medical school I would give every minister and his family free eye exams!"

So all eight went in that day to get their eyes checked at no cost. I heard Professor Ken tell this story with much gratitude and thanksgiving both to the doctor and God for meeting their family need.

**Thought for today:**
God knows what you have need of today. He is at work right now in your life to meet those needs—just ask Him!

# Day 15

EXODUS 3:7 & 8 (NKJV)

## God knows about your sorrows and can deliver you

*And the Lord said: "I have surely seen the oppression of My people who are in Egypt and have heard their cry because of their taskmasters, for I know their sorrows. So I have come down to deliver them out of the hand of the Egyptians, and to bring them up from that land to a good and large land, to a land flowing with milk and honey, to the place of the Canaanites and the Hittites and the Amorites and the Perizzites and the Hivites and the Jebusites.*

Are you facing some difficulties today? Let's face it, life can get tough at times. Maybe your problems are financial, social, economic, physical, emotional, relational, academic (if you are a student), marital, on and on the list can go. All of us in the human family have challenges we need help with on the journey of life.

Well, the Hebrews were having problems as well. For centuries now they had been in exile working as slaves in Egypt. The Egyptians, for the most part, had no respect for the Jewish people. They gave the Jews the dirty work and the grunt jobs. For example, they were forced to carry bricks and lay them fast and furiously.

*What a challenge it would be to live with NO arms or legs.*

But did you catch the end of verse seven above? God said, "for I know their sorrows." Thank God, He knows your sorrows as well. Not only did He know their sorrows, but in verse eight He gave the word that he was coming down to deliver the Jewish people!

Speaking of sorrow, Nick Vujicic certainly has had his share of sorrow. Nicholas James Vujicic is a Serbian-Australian Christian evangelist and motivational speaker born with tetra-amelia syndrome, a rare disorder characterized by the absence of arms and legs. He is one of the seven known surviving individuals planet-wide who lives with the syndrome.

What a challenge it would be to live with NO arms or legs. If anyone had a right to get bitter and belligerent, it would be Nick. However, his parents, even though sad about his physical condition, did not baby him and challenged him to be the best he could be in life.

Now he is one of the most famous Christian speakers in the world, speaking to thousands each year about how to overcome obstacles in life. God has also given him a supportive wife and four lovely children.

I follow Nick on Instagram. He has over a million followers, and his bio reads this way: "Motivational speaker, best-selling author, and evangelist. Inspiring millions with his story of faith, hope, and overcoming adversity." What a testimony!

**Thought for the day:**
God really does care about our sorrows. What is it today that you need to cry out to Him about in your life? Go ahead. He is listening to you!

**Hopeful Reflections:**

> *It is good that one should **hope** and wait quietly for the salvation of the Lord* (Lamentations 3:26, NKJV).

> Remember Whose you are and Whom you serve. Provoke yourself by recollection, and your affection for God will increase tenfold; your imagination will not be starved any longer, but will be quick and enthusiastic, and your hope will be inexpressibly bright.
> —*Oswald Chambers*

EXODUS 4:10 (NIV)

## God uses imperfect people

*Moses said to the Lord, "Pardon your servant, Lord. I have never been eloquent, neither in the past nor since you have spoken to your servant. I am slow of speech and tongue."*

Do you ever feel inadequate or not quite up to the job God has called you to do? This is how Moses was feeling when God tapped him on the shoulder to be the leader and spokesman for Him to the Israelite people.

However, we learn that even though God sent his brother, Aaron, to assist him in communicating to the people, God would not let him off the hook! We don't know for sure what kind of speech impediment Moses dealt with, but we do know he thought it disqualified him to be used of God.

I enjoy reading the writings of Dr. Norman Vincent Peale. With all the negativity in the news these days it is a breath of fresh air to read some positive material. He tells the following story about how God used a lady that was also imperfect.

*Always act as if the impossible were pos-sible.*

"Now let me tell you about a friend, Elena Zelayeta. I was a guest for dinner in her home in San Francisco, and it was one of the most delightful evenings of my life. The dinner itself would have made the evening a memorable experience. There were 16 courses, each one a masterpiece of Mexican cooking. As each course arrived, it was explained to us, its history, and how it was made. For Elena is an expert in Mexican cuisine. She had cooked every bit of this dinner herself – as she is totally blind.

"This woman once ran a beautiful and very successful restaurant in San Francisco. When she lost her sight, her sons took over the business. As she was sitting alone at home one day, the telephone rang. She groped her way to it and lifted the receiver. 'Your husband has been in an accident,' a man's voice said. 'I must tell you that he is dead.'

"Blind – and now suddenly her husband had been taken from her! She turned to the Scriptures, struggling in her darkness, reaching for the help of Almighty God with all that was in her. She told me that one day in the darkness, she felt a great hand take hold of her own and lift her up. She gained victory over her difficulties. She began to live a wonderful life. She has traveled up and down the West coast speaking to audiences of 1,000 or more women, demonstrating her cooking on the stage, cooking with the senses of taste and smell and touch. She has written books.

"That night at dinner I asked her, 'What is your secret, Elena?' Her answer is worth its weight in gold: 'Always act as if the impossible were possible.'"

**Thought for the day:**
Be encouraged today that God uses everyone that is available to Him—even if they can't speak well or even if they are blind. What can you do for the Father? Remember, you don't have to be perfect!

**Hopeful Reflections:**

> *Therefore, having been justified by faith, we have peace with God through our Lord Jesus Christ, through whom also we have access by faith into this grace in which we stand, and rejoice in* **hope** *of the glory of God* (Romans 5:1-2, NKJV).

The Spirit of God first imparts love; he next inspires hope, and then gives liberty; and that is about the last thing we have in many of our churches. —*Dwight L. Moody*

Exodus 14:13 & 14 (NKJV)

## Do not fear because God is near

*And Moses said to the people, "Do not be afraid. Stand still, and see the salvation of the Lord, which He will accomplish for you today. For the Egyptians whom you see today, you shall see again no more forever. The Lord will fight for you, and you shall hold your peace."*

Have you ever felt like you were facing such danger that you were not going to make it and end up dead? This is how the Israelites were feeling. They had a sea in front of them and hundreds of Egyptian soldiers and chariots behind them trying to kill them.

So they thought: This is it. We are going to die. There is no way we can swim across the Red Sea, and we are no competition for the Egyptian army with all their military forces.

However, God had something else in mind! He told Moses to tell them five things: 1. Don't be afraid. 2. Stand still. 3. See the salvation of the Lord. 4. The Lord will fight for you. 5. Hold your peace.

Along with these directives, God produced a miracle for them. Moses lifted his rod over the sea, the water parted, and the Israelites went through on dry ground. Then the Egyptians decided they would take advantage of the same miracle. God had other plans, so He instructed Moses to once again stretch out his rod; and this time the walls of water came back in place, and all the Egyptians drowned.

I know how it is to think there is no way of escape. After I graduated from college, three friends and myself decided to take a missionary trip to Alaska. On the way home, we were in a very bad wreck in Canada.

It was two o'clock in the morning on August 2$^{nd}$, 1983, when the driver of our vehicle lost control, and the pick-up truck flipped at least five times. There were four of us, which included the driver—

two were sleeping in the back of the truck, and I was a passenger in the cab.

We were on the Stewart–Cassiar Highway at the time and had not passed a single vehicle for about three hours before we had the wreck. I had just mentioned to the driver, "This would be a terrible place to have a wreck, no one would ever find us"—not realizing that 15 minutes later we would have one!

It threw the driver and me out the passenger window. Even though it was not a law to wear a seat belt in 1983, it is a law now and we should always wear one; but that night we did not have seat belts on, and it proved to be a good thing because it smashed the top of the truck nearly as flat as a pancake and we landed face down below where the truck stopped after landing on its top. It tore off the camper and threw the other two guys in the back onto the ground as well.

Realizing I was bleeding internally in my mouth as well as my face bleeding very severely, my first thought was: we are going to die here in Canada because no one will find us. But then God showed up! As soon as the wreck happened, He sent us a semi-truck that had a minister as the driver and a general surgeon as a passenger! I get cold chills even now thinking how God provided for us that night.

> *Realizing I was bleeding internally in my mouth as well as my face bleeding very severely, my first thought was: we are going to die here in Canada because no one will find us.*

It is a long story, but let me just say we rode three hours in the back of that semi to get to the first clinic. We all lived but were banged up, and one guy had to have surgeries and was in the hospital several days.

**Thought for the day:**
Does what you are facing seem impossible? Take heart, my friend, and don't be afraid. Stand still and see God work in your life.

EXODUS 23:20 (NKJV)

## Following the angel

*"Behold, I send an Angel before you to keep you in the way and to bring you into the place which I have prepared."*

As we read the first part of the book of Exodus, we find out that God worked several miracles. No doubt the biggest miracle was when He parted the Red Sea so that the Israelites could go across on dry ground, and then he let the wall of water go back and kill thousands of Egyptians.

But now Moses is trying to lead more than two million people through the wilderness to the Promised Land. No easy task! But the good news is God is going to send an angel to help guide him. How can you beat God sending you His own GPS system?

I have never seen an angel, but I believe they exist. It is my opinion they are still very active in our world. In fact, I believe God can still use them to guide us!

*While in the store, God spoke to her and told her in her spirit (not verbally) that one day she would be shopping there weekly.*

A few years ago, my wife Deb and I felt like it was time to move on from a ministry I was involved in—administration and serving as a professor in a Christian college. We felt like God was leading us to do parish ministry in a local church.

About two years before we left the college, we were headed to a family reunion about two hours away from the school where I worked. On the way to the reunion, we stopped in a Jay C grocery store, and Deb went in to get some food to take. While in the store, God spoke to her and told her in her spirit (not verbally) that one day she would be shopping there weekly.

She never told me about this experience until after we had moved two years later. We moved so I could serve as pastor at a church that was about 15 minutes from this Jay C grocery store. Yes, you guessed it, she did indeed shop there every week for groceries!

Did an angel tell her what was coming two years down the road of life? Maybe. God spoke to Debbie some way that day, and it may have been through an angel.

**Thought for the day:**
Do you need help knowing where to go in the future or which path to take? Serve God and reach out to Him, and He may send you an angel to specifically guide your way!

**Hopeful Reflections:**

> *And **hope** does not put us to shame, because God's love has been poured out into our hearts through the Holy Spirit, who has been given to us* (Romans 5:5, NIV).

Only when our greatest love is God, a love that we cannot lose even in death, can we face all things with peace. Grief was not to be eliminated but seasoned and buoyed up with love and hope. —*John Piper*

Exodus 33:13 (NKJV)

# God knows your name

*"Now therefore, I pray, if I have found grace in Your sight, show me now Your way, that I may know You and that I may find grace in Your sight. And consider that this nation is Your people." And He said, "My Presence will go with you, and I will give you rest." So the Lord said to Moses, "I will also do this thing that you have spoken; for you have found grace in My sight, and I know you by name."*

Every leader has rough times doing their jobs. Moses certainly did! Here he was trying to lead nearly 2 ½ million people through the wilderness when God decided to send him up a mountain for specific instructions, namely the ten commandments.

God is now very disgusted because while Moses is up on Mt. Sinai learning how the Israelites should live, the people are in the valley doing the opposite and having a party. I mean a big party. Like taking all their jewelry and making a molded calf to worship. They whipped out the food and drinks and were playing games. They were no doubt in the wilderness playing their own version of corn hole.

*But wait, God is a God of second chanc-es, isn't He?*

The leader, Moses, came down the mountain and found this frivolity; and not only was he upset, but God also was angry and hurt. So much so that God wanted to destroy them and start over. But Moses interceded on their behalf as we read in the verses quoted above. Moses had no interest in trying to lead this mass of people without God's help. Who could blame him?

God is a God of justice but also of mercy. Moses said a prayer and God answered; He was going to give the Israelites a second chance. God changed His mind and reminded Moses that His presence would go with him, He would give him rest, and that He knew his name.

Did you catch that, God knew His name? You know what, He also knows your name! Give that some deliberate thought. With seven billion people on the planet, God knows you individually. What a comforting thought!

I have a friend we will call Hezekiah* who is a very dynamic preacher. He is very gifted in speaking and can sway a crowd with rhetoric, persuasion, and skill. I have heard him preach before large audiences and have a dynamic impact.

Unfortunately, Hezekiah got off track and had an affair with a woman and was unfaithful to his wife. I remember hearing this story and felt so sorry about the situation and for all of those involved.

But wait, God is a God of second chances, isn't He? The great news is Hezekiah confessed, sought repentance from the Lord, went through the restoration process of his denomination and is back in ministry now being as effective as he ever was in the past.

**Thought for the day:**
Have you slipped on your spiritual journey, sinned, or made a major mistake? If so, don't forget there is a way back. God knows your name; and if you ask, He is waiting to give you another chance with Him!

**Hopeful Reflections:**

> ...*rejoicing in **hope**, patient in tribulation, continuing steadfastly in prayer* (Romans 12:12, NKJV).
>
> Christ showed us hope transformed into sacrificial love. —*Chuck Colson*

---

*Note: Hezekiah is not my friend's real name to protect his privacy.

# Day 20

NUMBERS 6:22 – 27 (NIV)

## God wants to bless you

*The Lord said to Moses, "Tell Aaron and his sons, 'This is how you are to bless the Israelites. Say to them: "The Lord bless you and keep you; the Lord make his face shine on you and be gracious to you; the Lord turn his face toward you and give you peace."'*
*"So they will put my name on the Israelites, and I will bless them."*

After all the ups and downs in the relationship between God and the Hebrews trying to get from Egypt to the land God had promised them, He still wanted to bless them. This blessing that Aaron passed on to the people would be good for all of us to memorize!

God is a jealous God, and He wants to be served wholeheartedly. The happiest people are the ones who accept Christ as Savior and obey and honor God with their lives. The Bible directly says that the way of the transgressor (sinner) is hard. So we should all endeavor to please God with our lives.

*This is how God oper-ates. So many times, He blesses us when we do not deserve it!*

However, God's blessing us is not primarily based on our performance. If that was the case, why would God be pouring out such a declaration of blessing with all that He had been through with the Israelites? The Bible says, "It rains on the just and the unjust." In other words, God waters with rain the wheat field of the atheist farmer so his crops can grow just like He waters the grain field of the Christian farmer.

Have you ever been blessed? One day I was in the office, and a large box was delivered. My first thought was, "Oh no, another large project to add to my already full schedule."

To my surprise, a preacher friend had sent my office a huge box of chocolate covered strawberries! Wow, they were delicious! The interesting thing was, I had done nothing to deserve them. But my family sure enjoyed them.

This is how God operates. So many times, He blesses us when we do not deserve it! One definition of being blessed is, "Being endowed with divine favor and protection." Don't you want that? I know I do! What a comfort to know that God wants to bless us.

**Thought for the day:**
Why don't you take some time today to reflect on the ways that God has already blessed you? Then ask God to give you His blessing described in the verses above as well.

**Hopeful Reflections:**

> *For I know the plans I have for you, declares the Lord, plans to prosper you and not to harm you, plans to give you* **hope** *and a future* (Jeremiah 29:11 NIV).

Jesus is the hope of the world, and the local church is the vehicle of expressing that hope to the world. —*Andy Stanley*

NUMBERS 22:23 – 25 (NKJV)

## God can give you directions, even by using an animal

*Now the donkey saw the Angel of the Lord standing in the way with His drawn sword in His hand, and the donkey turned aside out of the way and went into the field. So Balaam struck the donkey to turn her back onto the road. Then the Angel of the Lord stood in a narrow path between the vineyards, with a wall on this side and a wall on that side. And when the donkey saw the Angel of the Lord, she pushed herself against the wall and crushed Balaam's foot against the wall; so he struck her again.*

---

This is a captivating story about how God used a donkey that Balaam was riding to thwart the journey he was trying to take to Moab. Earlier in the chapter of Numbers 22, God had not wanted Balaam to take this trip.

Even though God knew Balaam's intentions were wrong (he intended to curse the children of Israel), he allowed him to go but placed obstacles in his way. Three times the Angel of the Lord stood in the way of the donkey, which caused the donkey to be diverted from the intended path.

Balaam got mad at the donkey and struck her with his staff. It came to a head when the donkey just laid down while on the journey. This made Balaam even more angry, so he beat the donkey again. At this point, the donkey had had enough of this beating and decided to take up for herself.

It says in verse 28 of chapter 22, "Then the Lord opened the mouth of the donkey, and she said to Balaam, 'What have I done to you, that you have struck me these three times?'" So the conversation continued until Balaam realized that God was doing him a favor by letting the Angel direct the donkey.

Have you ever had God speak to you? Probably not through an animal, like Balaam experienced, but more like in your spirit. God does care and desires to interact with us His children!

A few weeks ago, I received a gift of $800.00. I discussed it with my wife Deb, and we had decided where to spend it—that is until I went to hear a guy talk about church planting. As strange as it may seem, I felt like God spoke to me (not verbally but in my spirit) to add $200.00 to the amount and give the $1,000.00 to a church I know that is going to plant another church.

At first I was reluctant to do so since in my mind we already had the money spent! However, the conversation with God continued, and finally I mentioned it to Deb (knowing what she would say) and sure enough she commented, "Well, if you feel like God is asking you to do it, that is what you better do."

So the check was written, and I gave it to the pastor for the church plant and never thought any more about it. Then one day I went to get the mail and there was a card in there from an old college friend, and in the card was a check for $1,000.00. This is the only time I ever received any mail from my friend John Bauer.

*God does care and desires to interact with us His children.*

When I called to thank him, he said, "Don't thank me, thank God. I told God if He would help me sell my Aunt's house, I would give you money along with two other ministers." I told him, "You sent to me the exact amount I felt like God asked us to give away."

My younger brother James is a pastor in Michigan, and we thought why don't we share some of this unexpected money and send it since it is near Christmas. We did; and when he called to thank me, he commented, "Thanks for the money. There was a poor family in our community that needed some help. We couldn't really afford to help them, but we did it anyway. It is interesting because the money you sent to me is the exact amount I gave away to them!"

So God can speak through a donkey, but He can also speak to your spirit. I doubt He will ever do donkey talk again, but He speaks to the human family every day.

**Thought for the day:**
You are special to God. In fact, the New Testament even says He has the hairs on your head numbered. If He cares about that detail, He certainly cares about the paths you take and the actions you do. Be aware of how He may be directing you!

**Hopeful Reflections:**

> *...if you continue in your faith, established and firm, and do not move from the **hope** held out in the gospel. This is the gospel that you heard and that has been proclaimed to every creature under heaven, and of which I, Paul, have become a servant* (Colossians 1:23, NIV).

> You can look forward with hope, because one day there will be no more separation, no more scars, and no more suffering in My Father's House. It's the home of your dreams! —*Anne Graham Lotz*

DEUTERONOMY 2:7 (NIV)

## God does provide for His children

*The Lord your God has blessed you in all the work of your hands. He has watched over your journey through this vast wilderness. These forty years the Lord your God has been with you, and you have not lacked anything.*

---

The Israelites, like us, could be stubborn at times. God's original plan was for them to leave Egypt and travel directly to the Promised Land. However, they kept rebelling and grumbling because they had to leave Egypt. The Israelites served other gods, which was one of the reasons they had to spend 40 years tramping around a wilderness. In fact, that older generation did not even get to see the land that God had promised them.

In spite of this, God still loved them and provided for His people. Notice the last part of the verse above: "The Lord God has been with you, and you have not lacked anything." This is how God is: even though they were obstinate and at times rebellious, God was still providing!

He gave them shoes that didn't wear out. Can you imagine this as a Nike commercial? God also provided quail meat, manna (a wafer-like substance that had a taste of honey), a pillar of fire to lead them at night and a special cloud to lead them by day! No wonder He reminded the Israelites that they did not lack anything.

> *He gave them shoes that didn't wear out. Can you imagine this as a Nike commercial?*

God is still providing for His children. About thirty years ago my wife, Debbie, was pregnant with our first child. Our son, Joshua, was born on April Fools' Day and came two weeks early and tricked us! At the time she was pregnant with

Joshua, she was working as director of a nursing facility which provided a comprehensive health insurance plan.

Everything was looking up—a baby on the way and excellent insurance to pay for his birth. Then one day Debbie came home and said they unexpectedly canceled the health insurance at her place of work. Say what?! Our thoughts were, "Oh no, we will be paying this maternity bill for a long time!"

My employer had a "safety net" insurance plan, but the maternity part was undependable at best. The deal was, if your wife had a baby they would submit your name in an insurance type directory; and if someone felt led, they could help pay your hospital bill for maternity. I was thinking: No one is going to feel sorry for us. We will be paying the whole amount!

Thank God Joshua arrived safely, and he and Deb were fine. We were so excited to bring him home and start our adventure with children. In a few days they sent us the doctor and hospital bill, and it was $4,200.00. I mentioned to Debbie that just out of curiosity I was going to call the insurance plan my employer provided and discuss the issue with them.

When I called the company and explained the situation, the lady said, "Mr. Eckart, haven't you heard that we changed our policy concerning maternity?"

"No, what was the change?"

She went on to tell me their new policy paid $85.00 a month retroactively from when you first joined the program.

So my next question was, "That is great; so how much will we receive?"

She said, "Please hold for a minute while I check." When she came back to the phone, she stated, "You get $4,200.00!" Wow! That made our day.

**Thought for the day:**
In what ways has God provided for you? Why don't you focus on this concept throughout this day: "Your God has been with you, and you have lacked nothing."

DEUTERONOMY 4:7 (NKJV)

# God is waiting to hear from you about anything

*For what great nation is there that has God so near to it, as the Lord our God is to us, for whatever reason we may call upon Him?*

---

Despite all the troubles that Israel had in their relationship with God because of their disobedience and waywardness, God still had a deep love for His chosen people. In fact, Scripture indicates that Israel is the apple of God's eye (Zechariah 2:8).

They were a chosen nation that God wanted to be close with as an example for the other nations to follow. He wanted to be near them and give them the ultimate friendship that far surpasses any human relationships.

The great news is God wants to be near you as well! In fact, Christ died on the cross to get to know you. In the new covenant we find in the New Testament, Apostle Paul reminds us: "There is neither Jew nor Gentile, neither slave nor free, nor is there male or female, for you are all one in Christ Jesus" (Galatians 3:28, NIV).

In other words, God is waiting to hear from you now, whether you are Jew or Gentile. He is longing to be your friend; and by the way, "for whatever reason you may also call on Him!"

> *During the summer at times while playing in our yard we kids could hear Mom praying at her altar.*

I was raised by great parents. My father, Bob, was a hard worker who provided diligently for his six children and his wife, Ella. My mother, Ella, was a prayer warrior who would often call on God for reasons that concerned her about the family and other burdens that may have arisen in life. We lived on a farm, and she went over a hill on the back side of the property and constructed a homemade but sacred altar. This is where she would often intercede to the heavenly Father in the strong name of Jesus.

During the summer at times while playing in our yard we kids could hear Mom praying at her altar. One day I went hiking and found where she would spend time with God. It felt like I was on holy ground.

Don't get me wrong, she was human like all of us and not perfect. However, she did know and serve Christ and knew that for whatever reason she needed she could call on the Father by the powerful name of Jesus. She is now in heaven, but the aroma of those prayers she prayed still lingers over our family!

**Thought for the day:**
What do you need to talk to God about today? He is listening, and you can talk to God about anything!

**Hopeful Reflections:**

> *We remember before our God and Father your work produced by faith, your labor prompted by love, and your endurance inspired by **hope** in our Lord Jesus Christ* (1 Thessalonians 1:3, NIV).

> Simply by our proximity to Jesus, we can bring hope and life to people and places trapped in discouragement and despair. —*Louie Giglio*

 Deuteronomy 31:7 & 8 (NKJV)

## God will go before you

*Then Moses called Joshua and said to him in the sight of all Israel, "Be strong and of good courage, for you must go with this people to the land which the Lord has sworn to their fathers to give them, and you shall cause them to inherit it. And the Lord, He is the One who goes before you. He will be with you, He will not leave you nor forsake you; do not fear nor be dismayed."*

Are you at times not sure which way to go in life or when deciding about a future event? I read the other day that the average adult makes 35,000 decisions per day (several studies validate this number). No wonder we are tired by bed time!

Joshua could no doubt relate because he was facing a huge task. He realized that Moses was getting to be in the senior citizen club and Joshua was next in line to lead multiplied thousands of Israelites across the Jordan River into Canaan (the Promised Land).

Thank God, though, as we can tell from the verses above, when the divine gets involved it relieves stress and gives us hope for the future that we are going in the "right direction." How can you beat God saying, "Go this way"?

*He got in a tight spot, but then God showed up and went before them by providing a light bulb for their vehicle.*

Several years ago, my college friend Pastor John Croft took his family to be missionaries to the Czech Republic. He got in a tight spot, but then God showed up and went before them by providing a light bulb for their vehicle. Read it in his own words below:

"This story happened several years ago at the Czech/Austrian border. I was taking a missionary from Czech to the Vienna airport early in the morning. The vehicle we were driving had a headlight out and passing from Czech we had no problem; however, the Austrian guards informed us that we could not drive in Austria with a headlight out.

"No amount of protesting or pleading would change their minds. They instructed us to pull over and wait until the sun came up or turn around and return to Czech. If we waited, we would miss the flight; if we turned around, that would be deciding to miss the flight and make other arrangements. We pulled over, and I told the other missionary and the other two guys that were with us that the only thing we could do was to pray.

"Maybe the plane would be delayed. Maybe God had another plan. So we prayed. After a short prayer, I got out of the vehicle, opened the hood and proceeded to mess with the light to see if anything would work. After only a few seconds a guard tapped me on the shoulder and instructed me to move out of the way. He reached in and disconnected the wiring and then unscrewed the light bulb from the globe. When he pulled out the bulb, the headlight came on. However, there was no bulb in the globe, and there was no electricity going to the headlight.

"The guard held the bulb up and said proudly, 'Now that's police work!' I blurted out, 'No, that's God's work!' He shoved the bulb in my hand and said 'Go!' We shut the hood, jumped in the car, and we had low beam and high beam. It took two weeks to order the part, and the whole time we waited for the part the light worked. It was a testimony to many of the power of God to provide. He is our power source!"

**Thought for the day:**
When your way into the future looks confusing, ask God to lead you. After all, He is already into tomorrow!

JOSHUA 1:9 (NKJV)

# Be strong and of good courage

*"Have I not commanded you? Be strong and of good courage; do not be afraid, nor be dismayed, for the Lord your God is with you wherever you go."*

Have you ever been given an assignment and thought, "There is no way I can do this"? When negative self-talk kicks in, the fog of doubt can keep you from seeing a place to begin! You become paralyzed.

In the context of the verse above, God had selected Joshua to take over the leadership mantle from Moses in guiding the children of Israel. This was no easy task! There were multiplied thousands of people, and they were hardly a joyful group to lead. Since being delivered from Egyptian bondage, they had hardly stopped grumbling and complaining. They whined about almost everything. They resented Moses' leadership. The desert was too dry. They accused God of leading them out of Egypt just to kill them! Then they fussed about the menu. Moses was blamed for every hardship to the point they even threatened the life of their faithful leader. In short, they flat out rebelled against God!

*One day, while making a bed, God revealed to her that she would teach people around the whole world about Him.*

So clearly there was good cause for God to remind Joshua (the newly-appointed leader) to take courage! He was going to need it! God is saying to him, "Son, when the going gets tough, don't be afraid or dismayed, because I am with you."

Doesn't God tell us the same thing when we face seemingly impossible challenges? God, our Father, is the "Great I Am," and He will see you through the hard times of life. We can claim this promise if we are serving God, because He calls us to do only that which He will enable us to accomplish.

About 70 years ago, a little girl named Joyce was born into a home in the USA. She grew up in such a terribly dysfunctional family, it almost defies the imagination. Tragically, this precious child was raped approximately 200 times by her own dad. Although her mother knew about this situation, she covered up this terrible sin and crime to avoid shaming their family name. So sad!

However, the story does not end in sadness. Can you believe that Joyce discovered she had a wonderful heavenly Father and began following Him? One day, while making a bed, God revealed to her that she would teach people around the whole world about Him. She doubted the possibility of such a thing! How could she ever be capable or worthy of such honor? Her terrible past seemed to stand against her ever realizing God's plan for her life.

Then she shifted focus from her past to verses like the one listed above, and a confidence in God's dream for her began to take hold. Doors began to open, and she started speaking, writing, and teaching. Things progressed until she now reaches millions every week through her ministry! Countless people, seemingly trapped in terrible situations, are offered the same hope she came to experience. President of a large organization with hundreds of employees, she illustrates what is possible when courage and trust can triumph over fear and shame!

This not an endorsement of all aspects of Joyce Meyers' theology, but you have to admit her faith in God and focus on Scripture has allowed Christ to mold and reshape her thinking. She simply trusted God's leading in her life.

Not everyone is called to a world-wide ministry, but we are all called to be strong and courageous and to hold out hope for all who struggle with despair and heartache. If we stop focusing on our past, our limitations and our circumstances and tune our ear and heart to the promises of God, we can make a difference right where we are. If God can help Joyce to refocus and turn bad into good, He can help you as well!

**Thought for the day:**
God is in the helping business. He wants you to succeed and will be with you wherever you go on this day. Just ask Him!

**Hopeful Reflections:**

> ...*in **hope** of eternal life which God, who cannot lie, promised before time began* (Titus 1:2, NKJV).

> Outside of the cross of Jesus Christ, there is no hope in this world. That cross and resurrection at the core of the Gospel is the only hope for humanity. Wherever you go, ask God for wisdom on how to get that Gospel in, even in the toughest situations of life.
> —*Ravi Zacharias*

1 Samuel 1:12 – 15 (NKJV)

## Praying until you touch heaven

*And it happened, as she continued praying before the Lord, that Eli watched her mouth. Now Hannah spoke in her heart; only her lips moved, but her voice was not heard. Therefore, Eli thought she was drunk. So Eli said to her, "How long will you be drunk? Put your wine away from you!" But Hannah answered and said, "No, my lord, I am a woman of sorrowful spirit. I have drunk neither wine nor intoxicating drink, but have poured out my soul before the Lord."*

When I was a kid the saints used to talk about praying through—that is, pray until you push through the doubts, confusion, and lack of faith until you touch the throne room of God Himself! You get to the point you believe something good is going to happen despite how dark things may seem.

This is what happened to Hannah. She was getting desperate because she wanted a son. I mean she really wanted a son so much that she poured out her soul to God. She prayed with such fervency that Eli the priest (the religious leader of that day) thought she had been hitting the bottle. Hannah quickly informed him she had not been hitting the bottle but her knees!

*Even though Uncle Kelso loved the homemade bread, he felt like he should fast and pray for his brothers for an extended time.*

Later in chapter one of 1 Samuel we see that Hannah did have a son and she named him Samuel. This boy grew up to be used mightily of God for many years in Israel.

My Father, Bobby, had three older brothers that all had unique names. Their names were Uncles Kelso, Estel, and Creston. All the boys grew up in southern Indiana and in their teenage years got away from going to church and had no time for God in their lives.

However, Uncle Kelso became a believer and then got concerned about his other brothers. He became so concerned that he, like Hannah, poured out his soul before the Lord.

His mother (my grandmother) Myrtle was a splendid cook, especially at making fresh bread rolls for Sunday lunch. Even though Uncle Kelso loved the homemade bread, he felt like he should fast and pray for his brothers for an extended time.

God answered Hannah's prayers, and He also answered Uncle Kelso's prayers. All three of my uncles became Christians, and all ended up in Bible college studying to become ministers. My father has two sons that are ministers, and my sister married a pastor.

If you look at our family tree (from his generation until now) there are pastors, missionaries, parachurch leaders, evangelists, Bible professors, and a district superintendent. In my thinking, a lot of this Christian influence in the Eckart family goes back to Uncle Kelso, who was willing to pray until he touched heaven!

**Thought for the day:**
God is no respecter of persons. Just like he answered the prayers of Hannah and Uncle Kelso, He will answer your prayer if you pour out your soul before the Lord!

**Hopeful Reflections:**

> …*looking for the blessed* **hope** *and glorious appearing of our great God and Savior Jesus Christ* (Titus 2:13, NKJV).

> Where there is no hope in the future, there is no power in the present. —*John Maxwell*

1 Samuel: 2:7 & 8 (NKJV)

## God uses both poor and rich people

*The Lord makes poor and makes rich; He brings low and lifts up. He raises the poor from the dust and lifts the beggar from the ash heap, to set them among princes and make them inherit the throne of glory.*

These verses above are from Hannah's song of praise after God had given her a son, Samuel. She is happy as a song bird on Easter morning giving God praise for answering her specific prayer of giving her a child.

The praise song is 10 verses long and she covers various topics including God making people poor and rich. We could get into a long discussion about what these verses mean, but we do know one thing—that God can raise a person up and take them down.

*The encouraging news is that there is hope that even the beggar can be lifted up from the ash heap and made to sit among princes!*

God is never impressed when someone is proud, and He knows who He can trust with wealth and influence. The encouraging news is that there is hope that even the beggar can be lifted up from the ash heap and made to sit among princes!

The reality is I have known some poor people who were such a blessing in life by serving God and others. I have also known some rich folks who were faithful to God and helped many people on their journey of life.

We were endeavoring to finish a project here at our camp ministries. Through God's providence I got to know a family that has more money than you can almost count. After much prayer I made a request to see if they would give us $50,000.00 but mentioned that we really needed $82,000.00. My thought was if they would give us the 50K, surely God would help us raise the other 32K.

A few days after I sent the request, they sent the whole $82,000.00! Praise be to God. This was the first time I ever did a praise dance!

A couple of years later when we were endeavoring to finish another program, we needed $150,000.00 to finish the project without having to borrow money. I made another request to them; and after prayer and fasting and seeking God, on one cold January day they sent a check to us for the $150,000.00 that we needed.

**Thought for the day:**
Learn to appreciate both poor and rich people. God works through all people to fulfill his purpose.

**Hopeful Reflections:**

> *...that having been justified by His grace we should become heirs according to the **hope** of eternal life* (Titus 3:7, NKJV).

The only hope for this or any other society is to hear the Word of the Lord and obey.
—*John MacArthur*

 1 Samuel 3:8 – 10 (NKJV)

## God may use other people to guide us

*And the Lord called Samuel again the third time. So he arose and went to Eli, and said, "Here I am, for you did call me." Then Eli perceived that the Lord had called the boy. Therefore Eli said to Samuel, "Go, lie down; and it shall be, if He calls you, that you must say, 'Speak, Lord, for Your servant hears.'" So Samuel went and lay down in his place. Now the Lord came and stood and called as at other times, "Samuel! Samuel!" And Samuel answered, "Speak, for Your servant hears."*

You can't really blame Samuel for not knowing at first that it was God who was speaking to him. After all, he was just a boy probably about 12 years of age. He may have been lying in bed thinking about where he was going to go fishing the next day, not expecting a revelation from almighty God.

God sometimes uses other people to help clarify his direction and journey for us. Notice in verse eight that Eli (the priest) perceived or recognized that God was speaking to Samuel and coached him accordingly.

> God sometimes uses other people to help clarify his direction and journey for us.

One day while pastoring I was sitting at my desk in my office studying for the next week's sermon. The phone rang so I answered, and it was my supervisor, Rev. Marvin Hughes. He was serving as the district superintendent of the southern part of Indiana for The Wesleyan Church.

We chatted a bit, and I was honestly able to tell him I was studying for my sermon (glad I wasn't watching a rerun of a Colts game!). He proceeded to tell me some interesting news. He said something like this, "Pastor Mark, I was praying this morning and God told me that you are going to be the next district superintendent for this district." I was shocked and stunned to say the least!

After he finished with his prophecy, I commented, "Rev. Hughes, I have the utmost confidence in you and your prayers, but it seems to me that you have missed the mark on this one." Two years later, in March, I was approached about serving as district superintendent and was voted in later that summer. With God's help I have been serving nearly 17 years as DS. It is interesting that God used Rev. Hughes to prepare me for what was coming down the road in my ministry.

**Thought for the day:**
God doesn't speak through everyone, but he does some people. Be encouraged—God may give you a nudge of direction today by being in conversation with a friend!

**Hopeful Reflections:**

> *We have this **hope** as an anchor for the soul, firm and secure. It enters the inner sanctuary behind the curtain* (Hebrews 6:19, NIV).

Many things are possible for the person who has hope. Even more is possible for the person who has faith. And still more is possible for the person who knows how to love. But everything is possible for the person who practices all three virtues.

—*Brother Lawrence*

1 Samuel 7:7 - 9 (NKJV)

## The hope of crying out to the Lord

*When the Philistines heard that Israel had assembled at Mizpah, the rulers of the Philistines came up to attack them. When the Israelites heard of it, they were afraid because of the Philistines. They said to Samuel, "Do not stop crying out to the Lord our God for us, that he may rescue us from the hand of the Philistines." Then Samuel took a suckling lamb and sacrificed it as a whole burnt offering to the Lord. He cried out to the Lord on Israel's behalf, and the Lord answered him.*

The Israelites found themselves in a pickle. As was often the case in the Old Testament, the Jewish people had strayed away from God and His expectations for them. However, God was once again being faithful and using the prophet Samuel to bring them back to "rightness" with God.

From admonition by the prophet, the Israelites had agreed to put away their false gods and serve only the Lord. However, as is often the case, not everyone was happy with the decision to follow the true God. Notice the Philistines were planning to attack Israel, but Samuel cried out to the Lord.

The great news is God heard Samuel's cries and answered his prayers. That day Israel was delivered from their enemy the Philistines. The result was, as long as Samuel was living, there was peace in the land. The Israelites recovered the cities they had lost, and never again did the Philistines try to overtake the Jewish people!

This is how it is when God answers cries sent up to Him. One man said it well when he commented, "God answers prayer by saying yes, no, and slow!" But when prayers get answered in the affirmative, good things always happen!

A few years after Deb and I got married, we were so excited about getting our first new car. It was a new minivan because we were planning on having more children and knew we needed a dependable car for our family.

It was wonderful. It had that new car smell and was so fun to drive. But after only a week, I went to fill it up with gasoline one day, and after I paid for my gas and started to leave it would not start. So since it was new and still under warranty, I just called a wrecker to transport it to the dealership. He dropped me by home and then had to go another ten miles or so to deliver our "new" broken van.

The next day the dealership called me and said, "Mr. Eckart, we have good news and bad news; which do you want first?"

I replied, "Give me the bad news first."

The mechanic then stated, "Well, the bad news is your vehicle has about $1,500.00 worth of damage. The good news is we know what caused it!"

He went on to tell me that a groundhog had crawled up on the engine when the van had been parked by some trees earlier in the day. I went to get gasoline. It had chewed in two every wire it could find on top of the engine. Not only that, it had ridden about 15 miles on top of the engine by the time it got to the dealership.

The mechanic said that stupid groundhog was still alive when they found it, but it had burned its tail off from the heat of the engine. Can you believe they turned the groundhog loose into the woods? They should have sent it to hog heaven!

> "God answers prayer by saying yes, no, and slow!"

So my first thoughts were, I'm sure warranty will cover this freak accident. When I checked, they soon let me know they would not in that they considered it an act of God!

With that news I then called our insurance agent (I still remember his name, Mr. Clark) and asked him if insurance would pay for the damage, and he replied they would not. Wow! So now we were making payments on a brand new car we couldn't drive because some obnoxious groundhog ate supper by chewing the wires, and we were in debt $1,500.00 more dollars!

I then asked him to please check with his supervisor. He said, "I will put you on hold and get back with you." This was when in my heart and even verbally I "called out to the Lord." Your prayers don't always have to be long—just sincere and with the right motive. I prayed asking God for them to please pay the bill since we were in ministry and certainly didn't have the extra $1,500.00 in our budget.

In a while Mr. Clark came back on the phone and said in essence, "We normally don't cover some freak accident like this, but my boss said this time we will go ahead and pay for it!" Praise be to God!

**Thought for the day:**
Do you have an issue you are facing where you need divine help? If so, cry out to the Lord because He is there to help.

**Hopeful Reflections:**

> *Blessed be the God and Father of our Lord Jesus Christ, who according to His abundant mercy has begotten us again to a living* **hope** *through the resurrection of Jesus Christ from the dead* (1 Peter 1:3, NKJV).

> Don't lose hope. When it gets darkest, the stars come out. —*Unknown*

1 Samuel 17:48 – 51

## Conquering your giants

*As the Philistine moved closer to attack him, David ran quickly toward the battle line to meet him. Reaching into his bag and taking out a stone, he slung it and struck the Philistine on the forehead. The stone sank into his forehead, and he fell facedown on the ground. So David triumphed over the Philistine with a sling and a stone; without a sword in his hand he struck down the Philistine and killed him. David ran and stood over him. He took hold of the Philistine's sword and drew it from the sheath. After he killed him, he cut off his head with the sword.*

David had his work cut out for him. The odds were stacked against him for sure. The giant he was about to kill was some nine feet tall, David didn't even have a spear, and his older brothers and the Israelite army had zero confidence in him as a warrior.

However, as his brothers doubted, King Saul stressed because David would not wear his cumbersome armor (after all, the armor was so big David couldn't walk in it). Goliath the giant mocked David, yet he went on anyway into battle and killed the braggart!

Where did David's confidence come from? Early in the chapter he said to Goliath, "But I come to you in the name of the Lord of hosts, the God of the armies of Israel, whom you have defied" (v. 45).

> *Dr. Carson also tributes his mother for giving him a love for learning and study, but he says God delivered him from his terrible temper.*

We all have giants to face—some more than others. One person who had a host of giants to conquer is Dr. Ben Carson. A few years ago, my son Josh and I got to meet and chat with him for a bit.

Even though his giants were not nine feet, they probably seemed that way to him. Here were some of his giants:
- He was raised in poverty
- His mom divorced his dad since he was married to two women at the same time
- He was made fun of in elementary school as a dummy
- He had a terrible temper and almost killed a classmate

Yet his mother decided she was not going to let Ben and his older brother Curtis end up on drugs, in prison, or murdered. So she assigned them to read two books each week from the library, and they had to give her written book reports on each book!

Dr. Carson credits all his success (and he has had a lot) back to this strategy of book reports by his mom and God's help. He also tributes his mother for giving him a love for learning and study, but he says God delivered him from his terrible temper.

Here are few of his many accomplishments:
- A graduate of Yale University
- The youngest medical doctor (at age 33) to ever become the Director of Pediatric Neurosurgery at Johns Hopkins Children's Center
- Main doctor in a 22-hour operation (the first ever separating twins and they both survived)
- Author of three books, and a movie was made about his life
- Was a US presidential candidate and is currently serving as the United States Secretary of Housing and Urban Development

**Thought for the day:**
Do you know there is hope in you conquering your giants? "How?" you say. By trusting and asking God to help you. Then, don't get sidetracked by joy suckers, and work hard!

1 Samuel 18:14 (NKJV)

## The Lord was with him

*And David behaved wisely in all his ways, and the Lord was with him.*

---

If you read much of David's life in the Old Testament you know he, like all people, had ups and downs; but overall, he was faithful to God. During his lifetime he did commit some sins, but it cost him; and he also got forgiveness from God for these missteps.

The encouraging news is God still forgives if we fall short. The point this verse is making is that generally speaking David followed the ways of God. In fact, he is the only person I know of whom God described as "a man after My own heart."

In some ways, God is with all people. For example, we can't even breathe without God giving us oxygen to breathe. But God being with us goes to a whole deeper level when we do our best to behave in His ways.

*It was a privilege of mine to go spend a few nights with him the last few months of his life.*

I have told people often that my in-laws were great to Deb and me as we started our matrimony journey 35 years ago. They showed love and care for us but did not micromanage our lives. They gave counsel when we asked but allowed us to make our decisions as we felt like God was leading us. We were blessed indeed!

My mother-in-law, Frances Jones, is still living and doing well. She is a wonderful cook, and the quilts she makes by hand are beyond beautiful!

Unfortunately, my father-in-law, Meredith, has passed away and has made his journey to heaven. When he was younger, he did not follow God; but one day when plowing with his tractor (he was a dairy farmer) he felt God calling him. So he stopped the tractor and got down on his knees in the dirt and asked God to forgive him for his sins. From that day forward, he started following the ways of the Lord.

He was a good and kind man. Meredith also drove a school bus, and the kids he hauled loved him.

Life is good, but it is not always fair it seems from our perspective. Meredith suffered a lot. He had some 18 surgeries on his knees. This was back in the day when the technology was not as advanced as it is today. He got repeated infections, and one time I remember he had to lie 81 days flat on his back in a hospital bed trying to recover from his surgeries.

He finally had to have a leg amputated near the knee on one of his limbs. Even though his wife, Frances, did an outstanding job of helping to care for him as he got older, he had to have additional help.

It was a privilege of mine to go spend a few nights with him the last few months of his life. I did what I could to help him get back and forth to bed and even on occasion fry him an egg or two for breakfast!

I tell you this story to let you know that even though Meredith had many physical problems and suffered, yet the Lord was with him. Sure, Meredith had some long days and hard nights, but his faith stood strong in the Lord. He did not blame God, nor did he waver. He took what came with grace, knowing he was headed to a place where there is no more pain, sorrow, or operations!

**Thought for the day:**
What joy to know that we can walk in the Lord's ways like David did. Meredith was an example of someone who experienced God being with him even in difficult times. True hope comes from serving God!

"Dr. Mark Eckart has written a practical devotional book that includes a wealth of personal stories from Mark's life as a father, pastor and leader in the church. I've added this book to my daily devotional reading schedule and find myself looking forward to the inspiring stories which come from a life well lived – I encourage you to do so too!"

—Dr. Henry Smith
*Board Member of the National Higher Learning Commission*
*Served as President of Indiana Wesleyan University (2006 – 2013)*

"These devotionals are exceptional, and I loved reading them. Dr. Eckart draws from the lives of beloved Old Testament heroes to provide a daily dose of encouragement in *A Month of Hope*. I highly recommend this inspiring devotional treasure trove of heartwarming stories."

—Rev. Mark Wilson
*Author and Conference Speaker*
*Associate Professor at Southern Wesleyan University*

"Dr. Mark Eckart brings hope into the room with him. Even in difficult challenges, Pastor Mark always has a positive spirit and an encouraging word. I'm grateful that he has captured some of his favorite stories and hope-inspiring Bibles verses to share with us."

—Dr. Mark Gorveatte
*District Superintendent, Crossroads District, The Wesleyan Church*

Dr. Mark S. F. Eckart has authored five other books, worked as a professor and vice-president of a college, served as a local church pastor, preached numerous revivals, and for the last seventeen years, been the District Superintendent of the Indiana South Wesleyan Church. He and his wife Debbie have been spreading the "Hope" of Jesus to others in ministry together for thirty-five plus years. Mark and Debbie have three children and a daughter-in-law and a son-in-law.